Who are you ?

What do you want from your life?

Ask that question and once you know the answer write it down

Write down exactly what you want for your life

Your life vision

Your life purpose

And once you have that go
over it every single day

it every single day

create pictures in your mind

write down how you are going
to get that life

what do you have to DO to
claim that life?

Who do you have to become
to claim that live?

You see most people when
asked that question can not
answer it.

Most people when asked "
what do you want from life?"

Can not answer the question
they do not know what they
want their own life.

They are just wandering
around here, aimlessly.

Most people do not even
know what they really want
for their own life

And guess where people who
do not know where they are
going end up?

Some place they do not want
to be

That does not have to be you

The first key is to get quiet

Go in space alone and ask
yourself

Who am I?

what do I really want for my
life?

What do I need to do to live
my best life?

What is my purpose?

Why must I do this?

What example do I want to set to every around me?

Especially those I love those close to me

What legacy I want to leave?

Once you have that CLARITY and clear purpose you can get to work

Making every day your best day

Growing and evolving every day

Setting the example of a great life every day

LOVING the life you are living, every day

CLAIM that life today

Do not put it off any longer

You deserve this

Who are you ?

Have you really been living the life you want to live?

Or are you living the life others expect of you?

Have you settled for
something you do not really
want just so you fite in to this
world

Because it was easy?

Do you change who REALLY
ARE,to fit in with others

I am here to tell you that you
deserve better.

You deserve to live a live as
yourself.

To speak and live your truth

To live your fullest potential

Not only do you deserve it

But you owe it to the future generations to set that example

You deserve this to inspire others to follow their dream life.

To live their fullest, highest expression of themselves

You can decide to conform

You can decide to fit in

That is certainly easier

Certainly more comfortable

But you can also decide to LIVE your best life while you are a live

We do not get long on this
earth, in these bodies...

Why not make the most of it
before we go out?

Why not leave a lasting
impression on our family,our
loved ones and future
generations.

Why not set the example

The example of happiness

the example of a FULLY LIVED
LIFE

The example of love , peace
and true joy

That all come from being free
of opinions and just going for
what YOU WANT in life.

LIVE BIG.

You deserve this

LIVE BRAVE.

Others are counting on it

LIVE HAPPY

LIVE FREE

That is your true nature

But just these 3 things will
carry you if you let them

First and foremost knowing who you are being able to answer this question who am I and what do I want understanding that because I am connected to the source of all that is all that is possible, is possible for me that is who I am and what do I want?

I do not want to gust be successful in the world, I do not want to just make a mark or have a legacy

The answer to that question for me is I want to fulfil the highest truest expression of myself as a human being

I want to fulfill the promise

What do I want ?

You must have some kinds of vision for your life

Even if you do not know the plan... you have to have a direction in which you choose to go

I never was the kind of women who liked to get in the car and just go for a ride

What I have learned is that is a great metaphor for life,you want to be in the driver is seat of your own life, because if you are not life will drive you.

NUMBER 2

You must find a way to serve

Martin Luther King said that
not everybody can be famous
but everybody can be great,
because greatness is
determined by service

Now, we live in a world where
everybody wants to be famous
, and where we admire people
for just being famous...

We think being known brings us value

The truth is, all of that will fade in time

The real truth is that service and significance

service and significance that you bring to your service is that which is lasting

and if you look at all the most successful people in the word whether they know it or not they have that paradigm of service for many years I was really just happy to be on TV and people would stop and say " Oh you are on tv" yeah I am on tv

I like being on tv it's a nice job

And it was about the time that I received my honorary doctorate from spelman around 1993 that I went back and I took the long look at what it was I was doing on tv

And made a decision that I was no longer going to just be on TV but I was going to use tv as a platform as a force for good and not be used by tv

And I will tell you, my decision to make that significant change in the way I operated on television.

Using television as a service

Changed my career exponentially service

Using whatever it is you produce.

Your product as a way of giving back to the world when you shift the paradigm of whatever it is you choose to do to service and you bring significance to that

Success will, I promise you, follow you

Service and significance equals success.

NUMBER 3

It is so simple but so hard to do always do the right thing

Always be excellent people notice, think of how you notice

You go to Taco Bell and somebody gives you an extra sauce you notice you want to go back to that person

Because even at Taco Bell

Excellence shows itself.

Be excellent

Let excellence be your brand

So doing the right thing.

Even when nobody knows you
are doing the right thing

Will always bring the right
thing to you I promise you
that.

Why?

Because the 3rd law of motion
is always at work

For every action theres an
equal and opposite reaction

That is so true in all of our
lives.

Now you need to answer this question
question
Write down

1- Who am I?

2-what do I really want for my life?

3- What do I need to do to live my best life?

4-What is my purpose?

5- Why must I do this?

6- What example do I want to set to every around me?

7-What legacy I want to leave?